D1475332

LENTEN STUDIES

Prepare Your Heart For Easter

Marilyn Kunz

& Catherine Schell

6 Discussions for Group Bible Study

Neighborhood Bible Studies Publishers
P.O. Box 222
56 Main Street
Dobbs, Ferry, NY 10522
1-800-369-0307
nbstudies@aol.com
www.NeighborhoodBibleStudy.org

neighborhood bible studies

GROUP PARTICIPANTS

Name	Address	Phone Number

Copyright © 1995 by Marilyn Kunz and Catherine Schell

ISBN 1-880266-15-6
Third Printing, 2004
Printed in the United States of America
Cover Photo by Fran Goodrich

CONTENTS

HOW TO USE THIS DISCUSSION GUIDE

This study guide uses the inductive approach to Bible study. It will help you discover for yourself what the Bible says. It will not give you prepackaged answers. People remember most what they discover for themselves and what they express in their own words. The study guide provides three kinds of questions:

1. What does the passage say? What are the facts?
2. What is the meaning of these facts?
3. How does this passage apply to your life?

■   Observe the facts carefully before you interpret the meaning of your observations. Then apply the truths you have discovered to life today. Resist the temptation to skip the fact questions since we are not as observant as we think. Find the facts quickly so you can spend more time on their meaning and application.

■   The purpose of Bible study is not just to know more Bible truths, but to apply them. Allow these truths to make a difference in how you think and act, in your attitudes and relationships, in the quality and direction of your life.

■   Each discussion requires about one hour. Decide on the amount of time to add for socializing and prayer.

■   Share the leadership. If a different person is the moderator or question-asker each week, interest grows and members feel the group belongs to everyone. The Bible is the authority in the group, not the question-asker.

■   When a group grows to more than ten, the quiet people become quieter. Plan to grow and multiply. You can meet as two groups in the same house or begin another group so that more people can participate and benefit.

TOOLS FOR AN EFFECTIVE BIBLE STUDY

1. A study guide for each person in the group.

2. A modern translation of the Bible such as:
   NEW INTERNATIONAL VERSION (NIV)
   CONTEMPORARY ENGLISH VERSION (CEV)
   JERUSALEM BIBLE (JB)
   NEW AMERICAN STANDARD BIBLE (NASB)
   REVISED ENGLISH BIBLE (REB)
   NEW REVISED STANDARD VERSION (NRSV)

3. An English dictionary.

4. A map of the Lands of the Bible in a Bible or in the study guide.

5. Your conviction that the Bible is worth studying.

GUIDELINES FOR EFFECTIVE STUDY

1. Stick to the passage under discussion.

2. Avoid tangents. If the subject is not addressed in the passage, put it on hold until after the study.

3. Let the Bible speak for itself. Do not quote other authorities or rewrite it to say what you want it to say.

4. Apply the passage personally and honestly.

5. Listen to one another to sharpen your insights.

6. Prepare by reading the Bible passage and thinking through the questions during the week.

7. Begin and end on time.

HELPS FOR THE QUESTION-ASKER

1. Prepare by reading the passage several times, using different translations if possible. Ask for God's help in under-standing it. Consider how the questions might be answered. Observe which questions can be answered quickly and which may require more time.

2. Begin on time.

3. Lead the group in opening prayer or ask someone ahead of time to do so. Don't take anyone by surprise.

4. Ask for a different volunteer to read each Bible section. Read the question. Wait for an answer. Rephrase the question if necessary. Skip questions already answered by the discussion. Resist the temptation to answer the question yourself.

5. Encourage everyone to participate. Ask the group, "What do the rest of you think?" "What else could be added?"

6. Receive all answers warmly. If needed, ask, "In which verse did you find that?" "How does that fit with verse...?"

7. If a tangent arises, ask, "Do we find the answer to that here?" Or suggest, "Let's write that down and look for the information as we go along."

8. Discourage members who are too talkative by saying, "When I read the next question, let's hear from someone who hasn't spoken yet today."

9. Use the summary questions to bring the study to a conclusion on time.

10. Close the study with prayer.

INTRODUCTION

*L*ent, from the Anglo-Saxon word meaning "spring" or "long days", includes the forty days and six Sundays preceding Easter. (Since every Sunday is a celebration of the resurrection, Sundays are not included in the forty days.)

For its first two centuries, the Christian church focused on Easter Sunday, and there was no celebration of Good Friday. Christians probably followed the Jewish custom of prayer and fasting for the week preceding the Passover.

The period of Lent, as the church today knows it, originally was a time of special preparation for the new converts to Christianity who were baptized on the day before Easter. It became a time also when Christians who had denied their faith in time of persecution or had separated themselves from the Christian group through some other public transgression were reconciled to the church.

Eventually the period of Lent became a time for the whole church to commemorate the forty days of testing that Jesus spent in the wilderness before starting his public ministry, and a time to consciously enter into the meaning of his death and resurrection.

This series of discussion Bible studies is intended as spiritual preparation for the celebration of Easter. The six studies can be done on a weekly basis within the time frame of Lent. Bible portions used in this study series are selected from all four Gospels. For background, you may wish to review Jesus' teachings and the events recorded in Matthew 21—28; Mark 11—16; Luke 19—24; John 11—21.

DISCUSSION

1

How Does Jesus View the Human Heart?

MARK 7:1-23

What makes a person spiritually unclean or guilty before God, and what is the answer to such a problem? In Mark 7, the Pharisees and Jesus clash over this issue.

READ MARK 7:1-8

1. What reasons do the Pharisees find for criticizing Jesus' disciples? *They don't follow the traditions. They are impure*

    For them what is the standard of purity here?

Note: This was not a matter of hygienic cleansing. The disciples were eating with hands which were ceremonially unclean.

2. What accusations does Jesus make about the Pharisees?

*Note: Verse 5. During the period between the Old and New Testaments, a class of legal experts called the Scribes came into being. They amplified the great moral principles in the first five books of Moses (the Law), and broke them down into thousands of rules and regulations called **the tradition of the elders** to govern every possible action and life situation. The Pharisees,* *religious leaders who meticulously tried to carry out the teaching of the Scribes, were convinced that they had the correct interpretation of the Law and by Jesus' day these oral traditions had assumed a place alongside Scripture in Jewish life.*

READ MARK 7:9-13

3. How does Jesus illustrate the accusation he makes in verses 6-8?

4. What contrast does Jesus draw between what Moses said and what they say?

Note: **Corban**, *verse 11. When someone pronounced* **Corban** *on property or money, he dedicated it to God. This relieved him from using it to help anyone else, but he could keep it in his own possession until his death.*

5. What different things does Jesus say the Pharisees do with God's commands and with tradition (verses 8, 9, 13)?

    In your own life, what traditions or what new philosophies are you tempted to substitute for God's commands? *None*

6. How do the Pharisees judge their own and others' righteousness or standing before God?
    By their own interpretation of the law + how well theirs measure up to their idea of what the law means

READ MARK 7:14-23

7. Jesus emphasizes the importance of this teaching by calling the crowd to **listen...and understand...** In contrast to the Pharisees' view, what does Jesus say makes a person unclean? *Unclean thoughts*

8. What additional instruction does Jesus give the disciples about true defilement?

*Note: The disciples receive this explanation because after the crowd leaves, they **ask** Jesus to help them understand.*

9. Why, do you think, are **evil thoughts** the first on the list of what defiles a person? *Because the evil deeds spring from evil thoughts*
What is the meaning of each of the things that follow?

*Note: **Foolishness** (RSV), **moral folly** (NIV) is treating sin as a joke.*

10. How relevant to your own life do you find Jesus' analysis of the human condition? *True & very relevant, especially in terms of raising kids.*

11. If performing religious rituals doesn't make a person clean, what kind of cure for inner defilement do human beings need? *Recognizing the defilement from within inner healing through prayer & petition & receiving grace through the Holy Spirit. Works of atonement*

SUMMARY

According to Jesus' teaching here, what is every person's basic problem? *Not being in alignment with Gods aims*

PRAYER

O God, Father of our Lord Jesus Christ, we recognize that our right standing with you cannot depend on external cleansing if our defilement is an inward matter. We see that the cure for this defilement must deal with the source of the problem—our own hearts.

Create in us clean hearts, O God, and renew a right spirit within us. By your Holy Spirit enable us to think and do what pleases you. For Jesus' sake. Amen.

DISCUSSION 2

Who Does Jesus Think He Is?

MATTHEW 21:1-17

The atmosphere in Jerusalem is tense, charged with expectation. People in the temple keep looking for Jesus, asking one another, "What do you think? Isn't he coming to the Feast at all?" The chief priests and Pharisees have given orders for anyone who finds Jesus to report his location so they can arrest him (John 11:55-57).

READ MATTHEW 21:1-11

1. There is already a crowd following Jesus on his way from Jericho, including two men formerly blind whom he has just healed. What change in his mode of travel does Jesus initiate as they approach Jerusalem?

Note: Jesus' instructions here indicate careful advance preparations for his arrival in the city. **The Lord needs them**—*a password arranged with the owner of the donkey and her colt.*

2. Quoting from Zechariah, what does Matthew point out about the significance of Jesus' actions (verses 4, 5)?

Note: A king would ride a horse to war, but riding on a donkey was the sign that he came in peace.

3. Describe the crowds' response to Jesus' arrival in this manner. What do they shout?

Note: The shouts of the crowd are quotations from Psalm 118:26, part of the Hallel (Psalms 113-118) sung at the time of the Passover. Two hundred years before, the people of Jerusalem had carried palm branches and sung psalms welcoming the Jewish leader, Judas Macabeus, who had delivered them from their Greek conquerors and cleaned and restored the temple that had been defiled.

4. What impact does Jesus' arrival have on the city?

5. How do the crowds accompanying Jesus identify him (21:11; 16:13, 14)?

6. How does the crowd's identification of Jesus differ from Peter's declaration in 16:16?

    How does it differ from Matthew's understanding in 21:4, 5?

READ MATTHEW 21:12-17

7. The events in this section probably take place in the outer court of the temple. How does Jesus vindicate his actions in driving out the money changers and pigeon sellers?

*Note: Money changers changed foreign coins for those in which temple dues could be paid. Pigeons were the sacrifice of the poor, and Jesus' description of this place as **a den of robbers** indicates that the worshipers least able to afford it were being charged exorbitant prices by the merchants in the temple courts.*

8. In contrast, what does Jesus do in verse 14?

    Yet how do his actions in verses 12, 13 also deal with blindness?

9. At what are the chief priests and teachers of the law (scribes) indignant?

    What does Jesus say about the propriety of what is happening?

10. In your own life, or in your church, what things are in danger of crowding out prayer, and hindering the worship of God?

SUMMARY

1. In the events of Jesus' arrival in Jerusalem and immediately after, what do you see as the emotions of the crowds, and the emotions of the religious leaders?

2. Why do you think that some people today react negatively to *the wonderful things* Jesus does, and seem embarrassed by the enthusiasm that others have for him (verse 15)?

PRAYER

Lord Jesus, you came into Jerusalem claiming your kingship in peace. You came to the temple claiming your ownership and authority to cleanse and restore it to a place of Prayer.

Lord, do in our hearts what you did in the temple at Jerusalem. Cleanse from evil. Set our priorities right. Reveal your love and your righteousness to us, and then through us to others. We would receive you and serve you as our rightful king. Amen.

How Does Jesus Respond to Arrogance & Betrayal?

JOHN 13

How do you react to the person who goes out of his or her way to convince you of greatness? Or the person who is too proud to do a humble task?

Imagine walking along the road on the way to the Passover supper and hearing your followers discuss who would be the greatest in your kingdom! Jesus is on his way to death, and none of them understands what he has told them. Arriving at the supper room, no one is willing to take the role of a servant and wash feet dirty from dusty roads and open sandals.

This chapter begins Jesus' last conversation with his disciples before his crucifixion.

READ JOHN 13:1-17

1. What is the connection between what Jesus knows (verses 1, 3) and his becoming a servant to his proud disciples?

What can you know about yourself that will enable you to act with the poise that Jesus had?

2. If you were one of the disciples, how would you feel when Jesus gets up and takes the towel and basin?

   Who washes Jesus' feet?

3. Have two people read aloud the exchange between Jesus and Peter in verses 6-10. In handling Peter's responses to him, what does Jesus teach about cleansing?

4. How does this object lesson of foot-washing answer the dispute about greatness?

5. What avenue of happiness or blessing does Jesus promise his disciples (verses 13-17)?

   In what ways can you follow Jesus' example here?

READ JOHN 13:18-30

6. What does Jesus emphasize that he knows, and why does he share it with them at this point?

Note: Picture the men eating in the traditional reclining posture, each with his left arm supporting his head and his right arm free to reach the dishes on the table. Apparently, Judas is on Jesus' left and John, the disciple whom Jesus loved, on Jesus' right (verses 25-26). To give a morsel of bread dipped in wine to anyone was a mark of special honor and good will. In this instance it was Jesus' last appeal to Judas. To further understand Judas see John 12:1-6.

7. Describe the conflicting emotions there must be in Judas, the other disciples, and Jesus throughout this supper.

Note: Some time during the events of verses 18-30, Jesus uses the bread and wine of the passover supper to speak about the meaning of his death (Matthew 26:26-29).

READ JOHN 13:31-38

The Jewish people had been expecting God's conquering champion, the Son of Man, to bring the nations of the earth to grovel at his feet. But Jesus declares it is his **death on a cross** that will draw all people to him and bring judgment on the world (12:23-33).

8. With Judas out of the room, Jesus tenderly prepares his disciples for his departure. Why does he give top priority to his new commandment?

9. Ask two people to read aloud the conversation in verses 36-38. What is Peter concerned about?

10. How does Jesus' estimate of Peter differ from Peter's estimate of himself?

SUMMARY

1. What practical applications can you make to your own life from what this chapter teaches:

    about love

    about self-knowledge

2. From Jesus' dealing with his disciples, what do you learn about how to treat someone who is always trying to prove his greatness?

PRAYER

Lord Jesus Christ, we are awed by your gracious behavior to your disciples as you washed their feet, and as you made your last appeal to Judas. Deliver us from seeking to be greater than our fellow disciples. Grant that we may be recognized as your followers by how we love each other. For your name's sake, Amen.

4

How Does Jesus End Up With the Death Penalty?

LUKE 22:66—23:25; JOHN 18:33-40

Events are moving quickly after the Passover supper. Judas has gone to the Jewish authorities. Jesus and his other disciples are in the Garden of Gethsemane on the Mount of Olives when Judas arrives with a detachment of temple guards and officials from the chief priests and Pharisees. Judas points out Jesus by greeting him with a kiss, and Jesus is arrested and led away to the house of Caiaphas, the high priest.

READ LUKE 22:66-71

1. What two questions are put to Jesus by the Jewish council (Sanhedrin)?

2. From his answers, what case against Jesus do the elders now believe they have?

Note: The Sanhedrin had jurisdiction over all religious and theological matters. Its seventy members included scribes, priests, rabbis, Pharisees, Sadducees, and elders, and the high priest was its president. By its own rules, the council could not meet during the hours of darkness or on the eve of a Sabbath or festival. It was required to meet in the temple court, and death sentence could never be carried out on the same day given. A quorum of twenty-three members was required for a trial. The meeting described here, therefore, may have been an informal one hastily arranged to get a political charge that would carry weight with Pilate.

READ LUKE 23:1-5

Under the Romans, the Jews did not have the right to carry out the death penalty themselves. Previous mistakes by Pilate, the Roman governor of Palestine, make him eager to placate the Jews. Their leaders eagerly seize the opportunity to force Pilate to carry out their intentions to kill Jesus.

3. What accusations does the Jewish council make against Jesus before Pilate?

4. What evidence is there that they know their accusation concerning tribute is a lie? See 20:19-26.

5. What is Jesus' reaction to these accusations? See also Matthew 27:11-14.

READ LUKE 23:6-25

6. Trace the decisions Pilate makes (verses 4, 7, 14-16, 22, 24, 25).

7. What reasons are given, or do you see for these decisions?

8. What is Herod's attitude toward Jesus, and why is he frustrated?

Note: In sending Jesus over to Herod, Pilate may be trying to rid himself of Jesus' case. Perhaps he simply is getting a second opinion, and in the process showing courtesy to another Roman ruler.

9. What sobering warnings are there for us:

    in what happens each time that Pilate fails to act justly on what he knows

    in Jesus' having nothing to say to Herod who only wanted to meet Jesus to watch him perform some miracle

10. What steps can you take to avoid making the same tragic mistakes as Pilate?

READ JOHN 18:33-40

11. What does Jesus make clear and what does Pilate understand about the nature of his kingship?

12. Pilate offers to release Jesus to fulfill the custom of releasing a prisoner at Passover. From verses 38-40 and Luke 23:22-25, what do the Gospel writers emphasize about the enormity of the choice the crowd makes?

SUMMARY

1. For what claims of Jesus are the Jewish rulers determined to see that he is put to death?

2. In the hearing before the Jewish council and in the trial before Pilate, what do you observe about Jesus and his demeanor in contrast to those accusing or judging him?

PRAYER

Lord Jesus Christ, we marvel at your calm in the face of false accusations and unjust treatment. We see here the terrible results when people close their hearts and minds to you. Deliver us from commitment to other authorities. Set us free from ambitions that rival you in our hearts. We ask for your own name's sake, Amen.

5

How Does Jesus Face Death?

LUKE 23:26-56

In the crucifixion of Jesus, history turns a corner and nothing is ever quite the same again. Pilate and the Jewish rulers who coerced his actions are remembered now only because of their involvement in the events that led to Jesus' death.

READ LUKE 23:26-34

1. As Jesus is led from the Roman palace to the place of crucifixion, what incident occurs on the way out of the city?

2. What is Jesus' message to the women mourning his coming death as they follow him?

Note: Verse 31 - a proverb meaning here, "If they do this to an innocent person, what will happen some day to those who are guilty and deserve judgment?"

3. Describe the scene in verses 32-34. From Jesus' attitude revealed in verse 34, if we are his followers what should be our attitude toward our enemies?

READ LUKE 23:35-43

4. Why doesn't Jesus respond to the challenges in verses 35, 37, 39?

Why could these be considered Jesus' last temptation?

5. In contrast to the sneers and mockery from the religious rulers, the soldiers, and one of the two criminals crucified with Jesus, what does the other criminal say?

What is Jesus' response to this man?

READ LUKE 23:44-49

6. What unusual events does Luke record in verses 44, 45?

Note: **The sixth hour**—noon; **the ninth hour**—3 p.m. Since Passover was always at full moon, this **darkness** could not have been due to a solar eclipse. The **curtain of the temple**—only the high priest once a year on the Day of Atonement could go behind this curtain into the Holy of Holies, the innermost section of the temple, taking the blood of sacrificial animals to make atonement for himself, his household and the whole community of Israel.

7. What significance do you see in the comment that the curtain separating the Holy of Holies from the remainder of the temple was torn in two at Jesus' death?

8. With verse 46, read John 19:28-30. From what Jesus says and does at the end, what do you learn about him and about his death?

9. What are the reactions of the Roman centurion and the watching crowd when Jesus dies?

READ LUKE 23:50-56

10. The hours from three to six p.m. on Friday were called The Preparation. Between Jesus' death at three and the beginning of the Sabbath at six, what must be done if Jesus is to be given a proper burial?

11. What do you learn about Joseph from what is said about him and from his actions here?

12. Describe the actions of the women from Galilee (verses 49, 55, 56).

SUMMARY

Had you been one of those present at the crucifixion, what would you have thought of Jesus?

PRAYER

"O sacred Head, once wounded,
With grief and shame bow'd down,
Now scornfully surrounded
With thorns, Thine only crown...
What Thou, my Lord, hast suffered,
Was all for sinners' gain,
Mine, mine was the transgression,
But Thine the deadly pain...
What language shall I borrow
To thank Thee, dearest Friend,
For this Thy dying sorrow,
Thy pity without end?
O make me Thine forever;
And should I fainting be,
Lord, let me never, never
Outlive my love for Thee. Amen." ★

★ (attributed to Bernard of Clairvaux, c.1150)

6

What Changes Sorrow to Celebration?

JOHN 20

Have you ever been "surprised by joy" after some dark moment in your life? As wonderful as that may have been, it could scarcely compare with what the disciples felt three days after Jesus' death.

Mary Magdalene (Mary of Magdala) stood among others at the cross during Jesus' final hours. She was one of the women who watched Joseph of Arimathea place Jesus' body in the garden tomb, and roll a large stone in front of the entrance (Matthew 27:59-61). Early Sunday morning at the first opportunity after the Sabbath, she returns to Jesus' tomb with spices and perfumes for his body (Luke 23:55, 56).

READ JOHN 20:1-18

1. Why does Mary Magdalene react as she does when she discovers the stone has been removed from the tomb? See also Luke 8:1-3.

2. As Peter and *the other disciple* (thought to be John) run toward the tomb, what thoughts do you suppose are going through their minds?

3. When the two disciples reach the tomb, what do they see and what do they believe?

4. In contrast to Peter and John who return home, what do Mary's actions in this story reveal about her?

5. Describe Mary's encounter with the angels, and then with Jesus.

   Why do you think Mary doesn't recognize Jesus until he calls her by name?

6. What careful distinctions does Jesus make in referring to God, the Father, in the message he gives Mary to tell the disciples?

7. Why do you think that Mary is the first one to see the risen Lord?

READ JOHN 20:19-31

8. What change in the atmosphere of their gathering does Jesus' arrival create for the disciples?

9. How does Jesus convince them that it is truly he, risen from the dead?

10. By whose authority and with what power does Jesus send his disciples into the world (verses 21-23)?

11. What influences Thomas' progress from disbelief in the testimony of the other disciples to his declaration in verse 28?

12. How does Jesus' treatment of Thomas encourage you when you struggle with doubt?

13. What do you learn about believing from what John has written (verses 29-31)?

SUMMARY

What difference does it make to you that Jesus' story doesn't end with the cross but with the empty tomb?

PRAYER

Lord Jesus Christ, we join in the great wonder and overwhelming joy of Mary Magdalene and your disciples at your resurrection. What a transforming event!

We rejoice that the darkness and sorrow of the cross are turned into the defeat of sin and death, that doors locked for fear of enemies cannot keep you away from your disciples. With Thomas, we acknowledge you as our Lord and our God. Thank you for life through faith in your name. Amen.

★   ★   ★   ★   ★

Allow five minutes at the close of this study to read aloud the CONCLUSION on pages 35, 36.

CONCLUSION –
WHY DID JESUS HAVE TO DIE?

In these Lenten discussions, you have studied the setting and events of Jesus' death and resurrection. But you have not studied the reasons given in the New Testament for *why* Jesus came, *why* he died on the cross and rose from the dead. Consider these reasons as different members of your group read aloud the following explanations from the Gospels and New Testament Letters:

You are to give him the name Jesus, because he will save his people from their sins.[1]

The Son of Man did not come to be served, but to serve, and to give his life as a ransom for many.[2]

For God so loved the world that he gave his one and only Son, that whoever believes in him shall not perish but have eternal life. For God did not send his Son into the world to condemn the world, but to save the world through him.[3]

We see Jesus...now crowned with glory and honor because he suffered death, so that by the grace of God he might taste death for everyone...that by his death he might destroy him who holds the power of death—that is, the devil—and free those who all their lives were held in slavery by their fear of death.[4]

Now God's way of putting people right with himself has been revealed...God puts people right through their faith in Jesus Christ...everyone has sinned and is far away from God's saving presence. But by the free gift of God's grace all are put right with him through Christ Jesus, who sets them free. God offered him, so that by his death he should become the means by which people's sins are forgiven through their faith in him.[5]

Christ died for sins once for all, the righteous for the unrighteous, to bring you to God.[6]

You know that it was not with perishable things such as silver or gold that you were redeemed from the empty way of life handed down to you from your forefathers, but with the precious blood of Christ, a lamb without blemish or defect...chosen before the creation of the world, but...revealed in these last times for your sake. Through him you believe in God, who raised him from the dead and glorified him, and so your faith and hope are in God.[7]

In response to the death of Christ, Isaac Watts wrote:

> "When I survey the wondrous cross
> On which the Prince of glory died,
> My richest gain I count but loss,
> And pour contempt on all my pride...
> Were the whole realm of nature mine,
> That were an offering far too small;
> Love so amazing, so divine,
> Demands my soul, my life, my all."

What is your response to what you have learned in this study series?

[1] Matthew 1:21
[2] Mark 10:45
[3] John 3:16, 17
[4] Hebrews 2:9, 14, 15
[5] Romans 3:21-26, GNB*
[6] 1 Peter 3:18
[7] 1 Peter 1:18-21

* GNB. Good News Bible, Today's English Version

A POST-EASTER

PERSONAL STUDY ASSIGNMENT

During the coming week, read again the New Testament quotations in the conclusion (pages 35, 36), and answer the following questions:

Why did Jesus come?

What did he accomplish by his death?

What did he accomplish by his resurrection?

What practical differences do the death and resurrection of Jesus Christ make in your life today?

WHAT SHOULD OUR GROUP STUDY NEXT?

We recommend the Gospel of Mark, the fast paced narrative of Jesus' life, as the first book for people new to Bible study. Follow this with the Book of Acts to see what happens to the people introduced in Mark. Then in Genesis discover the beginnings of the world and find the answers to the big questions of where we came from and why we are here.

Our repertoire of guides allows great flexibility. For groups starting with *Lenten Studies*, *They Met Jesus* is a good sequel.

LEVEL 101: little or no previous Bible study experience
Mark *(recommended first unit of study)* or The Book of Mark *(Simplified English)*
Acts, Books 1 and 2
Genesis, Books 1 and 2
Psalms/Proverbs
Topical Studies
Conversations With Jesus
Lenten Studies
Foundations for Faith
Character Studies
They Met Jesus

> **Sequence for groups reaching people from non-Christian cultures**
> Foundations for Faith
> Genesis, Books 1 and 2
> Mark, Discover Jesus *or*
> The Book of Mark
> *(Simplified English)*

LEVEL 201: some experience in Bible study (after 3-4 Level 101 books)

John, Books 1 and 2	Treasures
Romans	Relationships
I John/James	Servants of the Lord
1 Corinthians	Change
2 Corinthians	Work – God's Gift
Philippians	Celebrate
Colossians	*Character Studies*
Topical Studies	Four Men of God
Prayer	Lifestyles of Faith, Books 1 and 2

LEVEL 301: More experienced in Bible study

Matthew, Books 1 and 2	*Topical Studies*
Galatians & Philemon	Set Free
1 and 2 Peter	*Character Studies*
Hebrews	David
1 and 2 Thessalonians, 2 & 3 John	Moses
Isaiah	**Biweekly or Monthly Groups*
Ephesians	*may use topical studies or character studies.*

ABOUT NEIGHBORHOOD BIBLE STUDIES

Neighborhood Bible Studies, Inc. is a leader in the field of small group Bible studies. Since 1960, NBS has pioneered the development of Bible study groups that encourage each member to participate in the leadership of the discussion.

The Mission of Neighborhood Bible Studies is to mobilize Christians to facilitate group discussions with spiritual seekers so they can find God as revealed in the Bible.

The Vision of Neighborhood Bible Studies is for Christians all over the world inviting people into small groups to question, discover and grow in their relationship with God.

Publication in more than 20 languages indicates the versatility of NBS cross culturally. NBS **methods and materials** are used around the world to:

> Equip individuals for facilitating discovery Bible studies
> Serve as a resource to the church

Skilled NBS personnel provide consultation by telephone or e-mail. In some areas, they conduct workshops and seminars to train individuals, clergy, and laity in how to establish small group Bible studies in neighborhoods, churches, workplaces and specialized facilities. **Call 1-800-369-0307 to inquire about consultation or training.**

ABOUT THE FOUNDERS

Marilyn Kunz and Catherine Schell, authors of many of the NBS guides, founded Neighborhood Bible Studies and directed its work for thirty-one years. Currently other authors contribute to the series.

The cost of your study guide has been subsidized by faithful people who give generously to NBS. For more information, visit our web site: www.neighborhoodbiblestudy.org   1-800-369-0307

COMPLETE LISTING OF NBS STUDY GUIDES

Getting Started
How to Start a Q Place

Bible Book Studies
Genesis, Book 1 *Begin with God*
Genesis, Book 2 *Discover Your Roots*
Psalms & Proverbs *Journals of Wisdom*
Isaiah *God's Help Is on the Way*
Matthew, Book 1 *God's Promise Kept*
Matthew, Book 2 *God's Purpose Fulfilled*
Mark *Discover Jesus*
Luke *Good News and Great Joy*
John, Book 1 *Explore Faith and Understand Life*
John, Book 2 *Believe and Live*
Acts, Book 1 *The Holy Spirit Transforms Lives*
Acts, Book 2 *Amazing Journeys with God*
Romans *A Reasoned Faith*
1 Corinthians *Finding Answers to Life's Questions*
2 Corinthians *The Power of Weakness*
Galatians & Philemon *Fully Accepted by God*
Ephesians *Living in God's Family*
Philippians *A Message of Encouragement*
Colossians *Staying Focused on Truth*
1 & 2 Thessalonians, 2 & 3 John, Jude *The Coming of the* LORD
Hebrews *Access to God*
1 & 2 Peter *Strength Amidst Stress*
1 John & James *Faith that Lives*

Topical Studies
Celebrate *Reasons for Hurrahs*
Conversations with Jesus *Getting to Know Him*
Change *Facing the Unexpected*
Foundations for Faith *The Basics for Knowing God*
Lenten Studies *Life Defeats Death*
Prayer *Communicating with God*
Relationships *Connect to Others: God's Plan*
Servants of the LORD *Embrace God's Agenda*
Set Free *Leaving Negative Emotions Behind*
Treasures *Discover God's Riches*
Work – God's Gift *Life-Changing Choices*

Character Studies
Four Men of God *Unlikely Leaders*
Lifestyles of Faith, Book One *Choosing to Trust God*
Lifestyles of Faith, Book Two *Choosing to Obey God*
They Met Jesus *Life-Changing Encounters*
David *Passions Pursued*
Moses *Learning to Lead*

Simplified English
The Book of Mark *The Story of Jesus*